AUGUSTE RENOIR

FELICITAS TOBIEN

Auguste
RENOIR

Artline Editions

Translated by Stephen Gorman

© 1988 by Berghaus Verlag — D-8347 Kirchdorf/Inn
English Language Rights: Artlines UK Ltd, 2 Castle Street,
Thornbury, Bristol. Avon, England
Printed in West Germany — Imprimé en Allemagne
ISBN 1 871487 26 9

CONTENTS

"For me a painting has to be something endearing, pleasant and pretty, yes, pretty! There are enough unpleasant things in this world without having to produce more . . . I know very well how difficult it is to create a lively art which at the same time is to be given the distinction of great art."

The few words with which Renoir describes his personal feelings towards painting are a key to a deeper understanding of all the works which the untiringly creative artist left to posterity. The striving for the endearing, pleasant and pretty is also clearly reflected in the choice of his motifs whose inner being he was able to detect with an almost tender intuition and to captivate on the canvas with natural grace. Pierre Auguste Renoir was born in Limoges on February 25th, 1841, the son of the tailors Léonard and Marguérite Renoir. When he was four years old, his parents moved with him and his brothers Henri and Victor and his sister Lisa to Paris. The family lived in humble conditions, and space was so limited in their house that Renoir had to use one of his father's workbenches to sleep on after his brother Edmond was born in 1848, as there was no room for another bed. Perhaps it was those difficult living conditions which contributed towards his becoming a responsible and hard-working person who regarded himself lucky to have grown up surrounded by such poverty. "When I think I might have been born to intellectuals! I would have needed years before I was rid of the prejudices and was able to see things as they really are. And perhaps I would have had clumsy hands."

The expressiveness of the hands played a decisive role for him, not just relating to painting, but also in judging people. It must have been a double torture for him later to see his own hands disfigured and crippled by illness.

Even in his childhood Renoir felt the irresistable urge to draw. His father's tailors' chalk and the floor in his parents' house which in his childhood served as the media for his first attempts at portraits certainly did not offer optimum conditions, but they proved to pave the way for his future success.

A considerable talent was also discovered in the field of music quite early so that the question of which career to choose later demanded some consideration.

Following his teachers' advice, he sang in the boys' choir in St. Eustache church whose choir leader, the composer Charles Gounod, was convinced that Renoir would one day become a famous singer. Because of this conviction Gounod gave him private lessons and also offered him a comprehensive artistic training. However, in spite of his love of singing, the thirteen year old Renoir felt a certain reserve at the thought of producing in public for the whole of his life. He also found painting more fascinating than music and therefore decided to abandon the idea of a career in singing, which Gounod had prophesied, in favour of an apprenticeship in a porcelain factory.

His master, Monsieur Lévy, had every reason to be proud of his new pupil right from the start, as Renoir eagerly dedicated himself to porcelain painting and developed such a great talent that his employers allowed him to work on more difficult tasks much earlier than was common in such an apprenticeship. He painted flowers, ornamentation and historical motifs onto the porcelain with an incredible speed. As his work was paid by the piece, this ability naturally favoured his financial situation.

Renoir spent every possible spare minute in the Louvre where he studied the works by the Old Masters with enthusiasm. "Apart from Watteau and Boucher I also discovered

Fragonard, especially his female portraits." The artistic impulses which he thus received were directive for his future life.

During his apprenticeship, Renoir took part in evening courses at the École des Dessins et d'Arts décoratifs and occupied himself intensively with oil painting. He soon realized that this would one day become his true profession, but he still continued with his apprenticeship, "apart from that I earned more than I needed with the porcelain. I was able to contribute when my parents bought the house in Louveciennes and would even have been able to exist completely on my own. That is not bad for a fifteen year old. But I enjoyed chatting with my mother when I came home in the evening. She was a splendid woman. Although she believed I could become a painter, she advised me to put some money to the side for a year before I began."

Mechanical progress had a negative effect on the porcelain industry. Craftsmanship was suddenly no longer in such demand as before, printing was to replace the artist's work in future. Renoir was forced to look around for a new field of activity. He was lucky as he was soon successful in obtaining a post as decoration and curtain painter in a curtain manufacturer's. He worked with the same speed as he had done in the porcelain factory and soon became a respected member of the staff there.

A chance meeting with the owner of a café, who wished to renovate his restaurant, brought Renoir his first commission for a mural painting. This was so well received that it was soon followed by more work of this type. "I painted about twenty cafés in Paris," he later told his son, "you cannot imagine what it means to have a large area at your disposal. It is exciting . . . Today I would still like to paint decorations like Boucher: to transform whole walls into an Olympus, that would be my dream."

When he began his studies at the École des Beaux-Arts on April 1st, 1862, he was twenty-one years old.

One of his tutors, the Swiss painter Gleyre, had his own studio which had an excellent reputation in Paris, and Renoir did not hesitate to enter this as a pupil as well.

Up until this point in time, Renoir had orientated himself around the art of the Old Masters, but now the contact with his fellow pupils Bazille, Monet and Sisley brought a decisive turn in his further artistic development. Although the lessons in Studio Gleyre carried on as before with the conservative teaching methods, the four friends — later to be joined by Cézanne and others — formed a community of interests, and calling themselves "intransigents", they endeavoured to bring new impulses into French art. They wanted to represent nature in its immediacy, in other words, as the artist saw it at the moment of painting. That meant that the ever-changing light conditions had to be included in the respective project, something which was, of course, only possible with a very precise gradation of colour.

In 1864, one of Renoir's paintings was accepted by the "Salon" for the first time. It received, however, so little attention that the artist destroyed it later.

His financial situation was catastrophic, as the money which Renoir had saved from his income as a decoration painter had long been spent. He moved in with his friend Monet who admittedly was in an equally bad situation. They managed to scrape an existence by taking on the occasional portrait commission. "But from time to time Monet obtained us an invitation to dinner, and then we stuffed ourselves full with larded turkey which was accompanied by Chambertin," Renoir admitted.

The "intransigents" found a suitable sphere of activity in the Fontainebleau forest where almost all of the landscape paintings from those years were created.

However, Renoir in no way neglected his work in the studio, it was his opinion that "Nature leads the artist into solitariness. I want to remain among people." He often went searching for motifs and had a predilection for painting figures. But flowers could also inspire him time and time again to new works. "Painting flowers relaxes my brain," he said. "I do not use the same spiritual effort for them as when I stand opposite a model. When I paint flowers, I place tones, try out bold colour values, not caring whether I mess up a canvas or not. I would not dare to do that with a figure for fear of ruining everything. And later I use the experiences which I gain from these attempts in my paintings. The landscape is also useful for a figure painter. Out of doors you are tempted to place tones on the canvas which you cannot imagine in the subdued light of the studio. But what a profession that is, landscape painter! You lose half a day to be able to work for an hour. Out of ten paintings you only finish one because the weather has changed."

During his "intransigent" time, Renoir could no more deny the technical influences from Courbet, Manet or Delacroix than the simultaneous — but contrasting — orientation to the classical-linear representation of Jean Auguste Dominique Ingres who he much admired.

In the years 1868 and 1869 two of Renoir's paintings were eventually accepted by the "Salon" after several of his works had been rejected.

Due to the Franco-Russian War he was conscripted to the army. He served from 1870—1871 in the vicinity of Bordeaux and in a cuirassier regiment in Tarbes. His task was to break in new horses for the cavalry. But Renoir himself first of all had to learn to ride as he had never before sat on a horse's back. However, he also proved to be very skillful in this field and enjoyed the work. As he remained spared from events on the front, he was not faced with any immediate danger through his army service.

Thanks to the care of his captain, who took a liking to the young artist and treated him like a son, Renoir even had ample opportunity to paint, and he also gave drawing lessons to his superior officer's daughter.

He was demobilized on March 15th, 1871 and was able to return to Paris where the sad news of the death of his friend Bazille reached him. He had been killed by a cannonball in Beaune-la-Rolande.

He met his other friends after the war had ended. The circle of "intransigents" became appreciably larger. Degas, Pissarro and Berthe Morisot also joined the group.

The first half of the seventies can be regarded as Renoir's Impressionistic creative period. During this time such famous paintings as "Pont Neuf" (1872), "Ballet Dancer" (1874) and "In the Theatre Box" (1874) were created, works full of life and colour nuances.

The acquaintance with the art dealer Paul Durand-Ruel became fateful for Renoir and his artist colleagues. The art dealer, who had an antenna for talent and who at the same time was very receptive to the new style, enabled the "intransigents" to hold many exhibitions in his gallery in the course of the years and also helped them in other ways. "I would not have survived if it had not been for him," Renoir reported.

But when the first attempt in the Galerie Durand-Ruel met with no response, Renoir, Monet, Sisley and Morisot organized an auction in the Hotel Drouot. The complete proceeds for 70 paintings amounted to 10,349 Francs.

An exhibition organized by the union of artists in their own initiative where 30 artists were represented with 165 works proved to be a complete fiasco. "The only thing which this exhibition has given us is the etiquette 'Impressionists' which I hate," Renoir commented. One of Monet's paintings entitled "Impression" had given the critic Louis Lerong rise to describe the whole group as "Impressionists". There followed malevolent animosity and shameful accusations. The artists were called revolutionaries and were mocked and insulted, the people did not make the slightest attempt to understand their intentions or to have discussions with them. On the contrary, the public and the press were in agreement that the "Impressionists" were obviously mad and that they were not serious artists.

Something which in those days was meant so ironically and derogatory has become in the meantime a firm and definitely positive term in the history of art.

In exhibitions of this type Renoir remained relatively unnoticed. However, in respect of his "Theatre Box" malicious tongues made comments such as, "Look at those grimaces! Where on earth did he find his models?" The artist, who was so self-critical that he destroyed earlier works of his which displeased him, found the criticism to be unobjective and unfair in this special instance. "Perhaps it was my pride, but I thought it was well painted."

The effects of such defeats also took on a form which threatened the artists' existence since the portrait commissions became more seldom. The public probably did not have enough courage to buy paintings from artists who had come into such disrepute.

In this disconsolate situation Renoir took spiritual courage from the self-assured Monet. Monet would not be put down, and Renoir attempted to imitate him. He worked unswervingly. The lack of understanding and ignorance of the new art direction were signs of the time. Renoir did not in his wildest moment regard himself as the revolutionary, which he was accused of being. "Painting is not a dream," he once stated, "it is firstly a craft which one should practise like a good tradesman . . . As for me, I have always resisted becoming a revolutionary. I have always believed and still believe that I am only continuing something which others before me have done much better."

In his words one discovers the unpretentiousness of the great artist who regarded himself lifelong as a craftsman and who rejected the word "artist" when referring to his own person. It was only in those few moments in which he was himself content with one of his colour compositions that he would playfully say, "I think I possessed a bit of genius today."

An important event in Renoir's life during this period of financial trouble was his friendship with the famous Parisian publisher Charpentier. They had known each other for some time, but now their friendship became more and more cemented. The influential publisher belonged to the few great admirers of modern art, and he proved to be just as bold as he was willing to promote. Towards the end of the seventies he founded the journal "Vie Moderne" whose production he entrusted to Renoir's youngest brother. The aim and task of this magazine was the support and defence of the new way of painting. Exhibitions were organized by the editorial staff, and Renoir was one of the first whose works were shown in an individual exhibition.

As well as this the Charpentier family commissioned him to paint many portraits, a task which he fulfilled with a very special pleasure. "Madame Charpentier reminded me of my childhood love, the models from Fragonard. The little daughter had charming dimples. I was congratulated. I forgot the attacks from the newspapers. I had models full of good will at no expense to me." The painting "Madame Charpentier and Her Children" is an excellent example of Renoir's exceptional talent of comprehending moments of mimic and gestural eloquence in a most charming way and representing them on canvas. The first traces of a gradual removal from Impressionism can already be clearly seen.

After his income had finally improved, Renoir could consider travelling so that he could get to know other cultures and carry on his studies there. His path first led him to Algeria in 1881 where — fascinated by the land and its people — he attempted to absorb as many impressions as possible. "I discovered white in Algeria. Everything is white, the bournouse, the walls, the minarets, the street. Above this the green of the orange trees and the grey of the fig trees."

In late autumn he also travelled to Italy. The stay there had an even longer lasting effect on him. Above all Raphael and his frescoes and the paintings from Pompeii in the museum in Naples gave him strong artistic impulses. "I was exhausted by the masterly Michaelangelos and Berrinis. Too much drapery, too many folds, too many muscles! I love paintings to have something eternal . . . but unspoken. An eternity of everyday life captured on the next street corner."

In Palermo, Renoir had the opportunity of portraying the composer Richard Wagner who only wanted to sit as a model for forty-five minutes. The speed with which the artist worked can be seen when one considers the fact that not only did he finish a portrait in this short time — it hangs today in the Louvre — but that he also completed several sketches.

In 1882, after recovering from pneumonia, Renoir undertook his second trip to Algeria.

In France, in the same year, he was again represented at an "Impressionist" exhibition after a long break, without him having given his permission. The art dealer Durand-Ruel had of his own accord given twenty-five paintings he had bought from Renoir to be shown at the exhibition.

The multifarious impressions which the artist gained during his study trips strengthened him in his attempts to find another form of expression which sought to orientate more around the art of Raphael or Ingres. He was certain of one thing, "Around 1883 I had exhausted the possibilities of Impressionism and had finally come to the conclusion that I neither wanted to paint nor to draw. In short, Impressionism led to a cul-de-sac, at least as far as I was concerned . . . Eventually I realized that it was too awkward to practise an art form which constantly forces you to compromise with yourself. Out of doors the light is more diversified than in the studio where it remains unchanged to all intents and purposes. But this especially is the reason why light out of doors plays too great a role. You have no time to give the finishing touches to a composition. You do not see what you are doing. I remember how once a white wall reflected on my canvas while I painted. I constantly chose darker colours but to no avail — it did not matter what I did, it remained too light. However, later, when I looked at the painting in my studio, it looked completely black. When an artist paints from nature, he is basically looking for instantaneous effects and nothing else. He does not make the effort to compose — and soon his paintings become monotonous."

He in no way wanted to decline into such monotony, but he found it very difficult to make the decision to turn his back on Impressionism, and this led at first to a severe crisis.

Renoir was searching for a very personal style, dictated more by sketching, and the search took a long time, too long for a person like him who was always keen to create, whose rate of work could not be outmatched. He was often impatient and doubted his own abilities. Many paintings from this period remained unfinished, others he destroyed. It was the only epoch of his life in which he — who usually had such a cheerful disposition — believed that he could find no way out, "I did not know where I was anymore. I drowned!"

In this desperate situation only one person was able to help him, Aline Charigot, who later became his wife. Aline possessed the necessary sympathetic insight to give Renoir sympathy, understanding and strength. "She enabled me to consider. She knew how to keep things going around me, things which I needed to solve my problem."

Eventually Renoir sensed that he was slowly approaching his artistic aim. In 1887, he exhibited at the "Exposition Internationale" by George Petit the first painting, just completed, which he thought would help him to his breakthrough — "The Large Bathers". To his surprise he was forced to realize that the public in those days did not yet recognize the great creative value of this vivid and aesthetically graceful work. "After three years of experimenting I completed 'The Bathers' and regarded it as my masterpiece. I sent the painting to an exhibition — but how I was brought down. With Huysmans leading them, everyone agreed that I was finished. Some even regarded me as not responsible for my actions. And God knows how I struggled!"

Soon after this the first signs of a serious rheumatic illness appeared, but neither the painful attacks of rheumatism nor the lack of success of that exhibition could seriously hinder his unflagging creative urge. Renoir knew that he had found his new style, that it was necessary for him to free colour from the influences of light and to limit himself to a few principal tones, in other words, in contrast to Impressionism, generally to simplify his palette. "To create wealth from little" was his principle. Again he believed in himself and in his work, and that was important for him.

Once, when asked about his methods and his opinions on art, Renoir explained, "I place my object as I want to have it. Then I begin and paint like a child. I want a red to have a tone like the ring of a bell. If I am not successful first time round, then I take more red and other colours until I have the tone I want. I am not cleverer than others. I have neither rules nor methods. Anyone can examine my material or watch me paint — he will see that I do not have any secrets. I look at a naked body; I see countless tiny dots of colour. I have to find those which bring the flesh on my canvas to life and movement. These days everyone wants to explain everything. But if one could explain a picture, then it would not be a work of art. Shall I tell you which attributes make art in my opinion? It has to be indescribable and inimitable . . . The work of art has to grab the observer, entwine itself around him and sweep him away. The artist imparts his emotions through it, it is the current which he transmits and through which he includes the observer in his passion."

On April 14th, 1890, Renoir married Aline Charigot who had been his partner in life for many years.

Gradually the artistic climb began. A large exhibition in Paul Durand-Ruel's gallery where 110 of Renoir's works were shown brought the eventual breakthrough. The State bought one of his paintings. Suddenly he was famous. In 1900 he was even appointed as Knight of the Legion of Honour.

Hard work, genius and perseverance had succeeded even if the path to success had been long and weary. The honours which poured so unexpectedly on Renoir and which should have made him proud hardly had any effect on him at all. He was only concerned with results, he did not demand fame. "Me, a genius? How ridiculous!" Those or similar words were his usual reaction to the exuberant praise of his admirers. The fact that his paintings now excited great interest with art dealers and museums meant for him the happy knowledge that he could offer his wife and three sons Pierre, Jean and Claude a materially secure future.

However, this happiness could not drive away the shadow which began to be cast on him and his family with merciless harshness by his illness. After a bicycle accident the rheumatic attacks began to appear at shorter intervals, and convalescence journeys to the Riviera only succeeded in affecting a slight improvement. Soon Renoir needed a walking stick. When this no longer offered a safe enough support, as both legs suffered from a progressive paralysis, he had to use two sticks and finally two crutches. With all his energy he tried at least to keep his hands more or less flexible with gymnastic exercises and by juggling small wooden sticks and balls. But the illness which in those days failed to respond to all medical treatment progressed mercilessly. His hands became more and more crooked, his arms were at times lamed, and one day he was no longer able to use his legs at all.

After having been confined to a wheelchair for some time, Renoir in his doctor's presence undertook one last attempt at walking. But afterwards he was so exhausted that he said, "I give up. I need my whole will for that and then there is nothing left over for painting. But if I have to choose between walking and painting, then I would rather paint."

When he could no longer use his fingers, he had his paintbrush bound to his deformed hands and worked on unerringly. He possessed the seldom found ability to express a relaxed joy in his pictures in spite of his painful illness.

Important sculptures were also produced in this period. For the manual tasks which Renoir could no longer carry out, he employed assistants who followed his instructions and concept.

Renoir suffered a further blow of fate in 1915, when his wife Aline died. The only consolation for him was painting, where a continuing artistic development could still be seen. Even when he became ill with pneumonia in 1919, he asked that his working materials should be brought to his bedside.

On December 3rd, 1919, Renoir completed a painting and said, "I believe I am beginning to understand something about it." He did not know that it was to be his last.

He died as the result of a congested lung just a few hours later.

ILLUSTRATIONS

13

14

15

Table I

Two Young Girls Dressed in Black. Ca. 1881
Painting, 81 × 65 cm
Pushkin-Museum, Moscow

18

19

24

Table II

Coastal Landscape. After 1900
Painting, 22 × 33 cm
Niedersächsisches Landesmuseum, Hanover

31

32

Table III

Two Women Bathing. Ca. 1918/19
Painting, 41 × 38 cm
Staatsgalerie, Stuttgart

33

35

Table IV

Girl with Hat, Sticking on Flowers
Painting
Private Collection

48

Table V

Jeanne Samary or 'Reverie'. 1877
Painting, 56 × 46 cm
Pushkin-Museum, Moscow

54

Table VI

The Pinned on Hat. 1898
Colour lithograph, 60 × 48.8 cm

Table VII

Girls Playing with a Ball. 1900
Colour lithograph, 60 × 51 cm

68

Table VIII

Bathing Woman Arranging Her Hair
Painting
Private collection

COMMENTS FROM HIS FRIENDS

CHRONICLE

The art critic T. Duret wrote in 1878 in "The Impressionist Painters":
Renoir excels in portrait painting. He does not just capture the outer characteristics, but also retains the character and inner being of his model in his pictures. I doubt that any painter has ever interpreted woman in a more alluring way. His quick, light brushstroke imparts grace, suppleness, devotion, makes the skin tones transparent, colours the cheeks and lips with a sparkling fleshy tint. Renoir's women are enchantresses.

G. Lecour, the sister of a studio colleague, wrote on March 29th, 1886:
On Friday when no one could tell him whether his paintings had been accepted or rejected, Renoir waited at the exhibition exit for members of the jury, and when Corot and Daubigny came out, he asked them if paintings by one of his friends named Renoir had been accepted. Daubigny remembered immediately, described a painting to him and said, "I am sorry for your friend, but his painting has been refused. We did all we could, we asked for the painting to be shown several times, but we were six against all the others. Tell your friend his painting contains great qualities, he should demand a salon of refused artists." Daubigny and Corot, both held in honour by Renoir, had recognised the quality of his work.

Paul Cézanne commented in 1902:
I scorn all living artists with the exception of Monet and Renoir.

The German art historian and mentor of the Impressionists in Germany, J. Meier-Graefe, reported on a visit to Renoir in spring 1911:
He sat alone in a large, bright room at an empty table. The frail figure of skin and bones did not take up much room and did not move. It appeared to me that he had already sat like this for many hours and that he often sat so motionless there. His face was like the dried up expression of the Pope on the Tizian in Naples, it was also sharpened by age, just as intelligent, but without the lurking insidiousness and uneasiness. He looked in a relaxed fashion through the big window onto the hills in front of the sea and allowed the sun to shine on him. He did not turn round as I entered the room and did not hear much of my veneration. The sun seemed to say more to him.

Pierre Bonnard said in 1913:
Renoir gave me courage when I began with my illustrations. As well as the gratitude which I owe him for this, I also acknowledge my wonder and reverence for his genius.

Ambroise Vollard, Renoir's art dealer, conveyed Renoir's comments in 1920:
Around 1883 there was a sort of break in my work. I had gone to the limits of Impressionism and came to the conclusion that I could neither paint nor draw. With one word, I was in a cul-de-sac . . .

Henri de Régnier reported in 1923:
I saw Renoir for the first time with Stephane Mallarmé. He sat on the small cane settee where Whistler and Odilon Redon often sat. It was the seat which was normally reserved for guests of honour. Mallarmé sat on the rocking chair which rocked beside the tiled stove, or he stood with the white or red clay pipe in his hand. The other guests moved their chairs to the table in the middle which was dominated by the hanging lamp. On the table there were grog glasses and the Chinese clay pot which contained tobacco. This room, which served the poet as a dining room and in which Lilith, his black cat prowled around, was furnished with a sideboard of polished wood which was decorated with peasant pottery. In a corner, raised on a pedestal, was a sort of Tahitian idol which Gauguin had carved. On the wall hung several paintings; Manet's portrait of Mallarmé and — also from Manet — a pastel which represented a scene from Hamlet with, I believe, the tragic actor Rouvière. This pastel hung for a long time above the small settee; then it was replaced by a landscape by Claude Monet and by a charming beach sketch by Berthe Morisot . . .

Renoir was neither silent like Redon nor a talker like Whistler. He was just, as it seemed to me at this first meeting, a person with a thin body, a thin face and unusually nervous. I remember a restless and intelligent face, full of delicacy, in which attentive eyes watched. Simple clothes and simple behaviour. Renoir had shortly before made a portrait of Mallarmé which, by the way, was not very like him and which was more a symbol of the painter's friendship with the poet than a finished work of art. Between both of them existed a relationship which, if not intimate, was at least cordial. This friendship probably began in Manet's studio where Mallarmé was a constant guest.

These heartfelt words came from Maurice Denis:
A whole life of quiet work without emphasis, a beautiful sincere life of a true painter. Idealist? Naturalist? As you wish. He understood how to limit himself to conveying his special personal artistic stimulations, all of nature and the complete dream in a special personal expressive manner; he composed wonderful women and bouquets of flowers with the joys of his eyes. And as he had a big heart and a straightforward will, he only made very beautiful things.

Hans Gaber wrote of Renoir in 1943:
Even Renoir was not successful in everything, but he succeeded in many things, unusually many. The artist only experienced one real crisis when he detached himself from Impressionism. It was the only time that he sought for long without finding, began without completing, started and destroyed and sometimes almost despaired. But when he found the new form, he again became the old, stalwart, passionate worker who was admittedly not always satisfied, and who did not experience any major interruption as a creative artist for the rest of his life.

Concluding one of the few comments, in which Renoir himself allows an insight into his work:

Painting flowers relaxes my brain. I do not use the same spiritual effort as when I stand opposite a model. When I paint flowers, I place tones, try out bold colour values, not caring whether I ruin the canvas or not. I would not dare to do this with a figure for fear of ruining everything. And later I use the experiences which I gain from these attempts in my paintings. The landscape is also useful to a figure painter. Out of doors you are tempted to place tones on the canvas which you could not imagine in the subdued light of the studio. But what a profession that is, landscape painter! You lose a half a day to be able to work for an hour. Out of ten paintings you complete one because the weather has changed. You paint a sun effect and what happens? It rains. You make a few clouds in the sky: the wind blows them away and so on.

The art dealer Ambroise Vollard had Renoir tell him how he came to paint the memorable Wagner portrait:

I was in Naples, when I received a letter from Wagner fans. They begged me to do everything I could so that I could at least bring a sketch of Wagner back with me. I decided to travel to Palermo where Wagner was staying at the time. He was not to be disturbed as he was working on the orchestra score for Parsifal. But by a lucky chance I was introduced to him. His first words were, "I only have half an hour for you". He obviously hoped to be rid of me with this. But I took him at his word. While I was working, I told him about Paris. He was most annoyed with the French and did not try to hide his feelings. I told him that the spiritual aristocracy was for him, which flattered him.

After a twenty-five minute sitting he rose brusquely, "That is enough, I am tired." I had had sufficient time to complete my study.

I used to like Wagner a lot. That certain air of passion which emanates from his music had a hold of me. But one day a friend took me to Bayreuth, and I must admit that I was incredibly bored.

These Valkyrien calls are good for a short time, but when it goes on for six hours, it drives you crazy.

Therefore I could not stand it for long in Bayreuth. After three days I had had enough and I felt that I had to compensate myself with something fine. I took the morning train to Dresden to see Vermeer van Delft's great painting "The Courtesan".

1841	In the year in which Renoir is born late Romantic art is in its hayday. In the previous year the German master of Romanticism, C. D. Friedrich, had died. Other artists belonging to Renoir's generation include Paul Cézanne (born 1839), Claude Monet and the sculptor Auguste Rodin (born 1840).
1854	Renoir begins his apprenticeship as a porcelain painter.
1862	Renoir enrolls in the École des Beaux Arts to become a painter. Fellow pupils in the Studio Gleyre are Monet, Bazille and Sisley. Cézanne also appears to have tried to enrol in the Studio Gleyre, but unsuccessfully.
1864	Renoir paints together with Diaz in the Chailly woods.
1865	Sees the memorable sailing excursion on the Seine to Le Havre which he undertakes together with Sisley.
1868	The painting "Lise" is accepted by the Salon where it is very successful.
1870	In 1869 and 1870, paintings from Renoir are exhibited in the Salon as well. He is called up for military service.
1873	This is the year when the artist finally achieves a financial breakthrough. Durand-Ruel notices him and buys the first paintings. Renoir is eventually able to rent a spacious studio in Montmartre. As his paintings are rejected by the Salon, he exhibits in the Salon des Réfusés which is held this year.
1874	The young Impressionists begin to organize themselves. Renoir is actively involved. He shows seven paintings in the first Impressionist exhibition.
1875	Monet, Renoir, Sisley and Berthe Morisot organize an auction in the Hotel Drouot. Renoir's paintings only fetch relatively low prices.
1876	In the second Impressionist exhibition, Renoir shows fifteen works. Renoir is also one of the most active painters in the third exhibition in
1877	where he displays 22 works. He also takes part in the second auction arranged by the friends. Again his prices are incredibly low. Admittedly the prices which his friends achieve are not much higher.
1879	Renoir's painting "Madame Charpentier and Her Children" which is exhibited in the Salon receives the highest praise. Among the circle of friends, Renoir's decision to send paintings to the Salon and no longer take part in the Impressionist exhibitions is bitterly resented. Renoir justifies himself, "In Paris there are hardly fifteen art lovers who would be capable of acknowledging an artist who remains outside the Salon. My delivery to the Salon is for purely financial reasons. It is as with certain medicines: even if it doesn't do any good, it most certainly cannot do any harm."

The journal "La Vie Moderne", published by Madame Charpentier's husband has a very good article on Renoir. Simultaneously an exhibition is shown in the publisher's premises. Renoir uses his influence for Alfred Sisley, who is in great difficulties, to enable him also to hold an exhibition in the publishing offices of La Vie Moderne, but it takes till 1881 before such an exhibition is dedicated to him.

1882   Renoir again takes part in the penultimate Impressionist exhibition with 25 pictures, parallel to this he exhibits — as in the previous years — in the Salon. Durand-Ruel is co-organizer of this exhibition. He has championed the Impressionists for many years. Now the difficult times bring his house to the verge of collapse.

1883   Durand-Ruel holds a special exhibition for Renoir, he also organizes exhibitions in England, Belgium and Germany where Renoir's paintings are shown. Renoir travels to southern France with Monet where they stay for a short time with Cézanne who lived in Aix and L'Estaque.

1884   In this year, Renoir detaches himself from his friends, seeking gropingly for new stylistic elements. His Impressionist period is over. He seeks to give his paintings a new mainstay until the following year.

1885   He can satisfactorily determine that he has found his new and individual path to painting. That summer he paints with Cézanne in La Roche Guyon.

1886   His inner consolidation is followed by outer achievement: He successfully exhibits paintings with the newly founded group "Les Vingt" in Brussels. He takes part in the "Exposition Internationale" by Petit, the very successful rival of Durand-Ruel, although he still keeps a good relationship with him and continues to work for him as opposed to Monet who also exhibits with Petit, but separates from Durand-Ruel in dissatisfaction. Renoir does not take part in the last united exhibition of the Impressionists where only a few of the old friends are represented. Probably because he sees himself as being in direct contrast to Seurat and Signac who, with their pointillistic painting, had been accepted in the circle of exhibitors at Pissarro's insistence. The first large Impressionist exhibition in New York, organized by Durand-Ruel, is a great success, especially the works by Renoir.

1887   Renoir's central work, the first large picture which he painted after his break with the Impressionists, "The Large Bathers", is exhibited with immense success in Petit's "Exposition Internationale". Apart from Renoir, Pissarro, Monet, Sisley and Berthe Morisot also take part.

1888   Monet changes from Durand-Ruel to Boussod and Valadon where he is under the care of Theo van Gogh, Vincent's brother. Renoir, on the other hand, remains true to his long-standing art dealer although his financial situation appeared very insecure for quite some time. While visiting Cézanne, Renoir becomes very ill and has to remain in L'Estaque for several months, cared for by his friend Cézanne. Later in the year he moves to Martigues where he begins to suffer from a painful neuralgia.

1889   Renoir again spends a lot of time with Cézanne in Aix. Monet organizes a collection to amass enough money to buy Monet's main work "Olympia". With a lot of effort, he succeeds in obtaining the money from the circle of friends. The painting is then donated to the Louvre.

1890   Renoir exhibits for the last time in the Salon. Berthe Morisot spends the summer in Mézy where Renoir visits her often. He also visits her in the following summer.

1892   This year sees also the breakthrough for Renoir's painting colleague Pissarro. A large exhibition by Durand-Ruel is his first great success and enables him time to breathe after a life full of privation. Renoir also has a large exhibition in the same house and also a great deal of success, including the first purchases by the State.

1893   In this year Renoir receives an honourable but time-consuming task: Gustave Caillebotte, a friend and customer from the early days dies and leaves his important Impressionist collection to the State. The will names Renoir as executor of the estate.

1895   Renoir's friend of long-standing and colleague from the Impressionist circle, Berthe Morisot, dies.

1896   Renoir travels to Bayreuth to get to know Wagner.

1897   The works from Caillebotte's unique collection are finally integrated into the French museums. Renoir's task as executor of the estate is finished.

1898   The first signs of Renoir's rheumatism are noticed. The illness eventually forces a drastic change in his lifestyle.

1903   Renoir moves to Cagnes for health reasons, as the mild Mediterranean climate makes his suffering more bearable. Renoir's move to the south of France should be counted among the most important events in his life. Again his work glows with new colours in an intoxicated wealth of warm hues.

1905   Renoir is housebound by the seriousness of his illness

1909   and only leaves his house in summer to stay in sanatoria.

1910   During a short phase of improvement in his illness he is able to make a lengthy journey which takes him to Munich.

1912   A comprehensive Renoir exhibition is shown at Bernheim's in Paris.

1919   A few months before his death, while travelling to another sanatorium, he is able to visit the newly arranged collection of modern art in the Louvre in a wheelchair, attentively accompanied by high dignitaries of the French nation.

LIST OF ILLUSTRATIONS

On the Terrace. 1881   24
Painting, 100 × 80 cm
Art Institute, Chicago

Coastal Landscape. After 1900   Table II
Painting, 22 × 33 cm
Niedersächsisches Landesmuseum, Hanover

On the Beach of Berneval. 1892   25
Etching, 18 × 14 cm

Young Girl on the Flower Meadow.   26
Date of origin unknown
Painting, 20.5 × 31.5 cm
Kunstmuseum, Basel

Woman with Mirror. Ca. 1912   27
Painting, 60 × 47 cm
Musée des Beaux-Arts, Rouen

Two Women. 1890   28
Black crayon and pastel
Archiv für Kunst und Geschichte, Berlin

In the Theatre. 1880   29
Painting, 41.5 × 32.5 cm
Staatsgalerie, Stuttgart

Woman Bathing. 1905   30
Lithograph, 31.5 × 26.5 cm

Two Women Bathing. 1895   31
Etching, 26.2 × 24.1 cm

Woman Bathing. 1895   32
Painting, 81 × 60 cm
Private collection, Fribourg

Two Women Bathing. Ca. 1918/19   Table III
Painting, 41 × 38 cm
Staatsgalerie, Stuttgart

Sitting Woman. 1906   33
Etching, 18.8 × 14.9 cm

La Grenouillère. 1869   34
Painting, 62 × 90 cm
Collection Oskar Reinhart, Winterthur

Portrait of Irene
Royal Academy of Arts
London.

Photographic acknowledgements
Unless otherwise stated, the colour photographs were kindly
supplied by the museums and collections.
PP. 18, 24, 40, 67, 69, 74: Scala, Florence.
PP. 19, 21, 26, 27, 32, 37, 42, 45, 48, 50, 51, 56, 59, 64,
72, 73, 75, 76: Giraudon, Paris.
PP. 35, 61: Blauel, Munich.
p. 66: Bergerhausen, Mannheim.
p. 41: Bildarchiv Bruckmann, Munich.
Tbl. I, IV, V, VIII: Colorphoto Hinz, Allschwil.